THE ULTIMATE RAGDOLL CARE GUIDE FOR BEGINNERS

NUERDIAS HUUPKANSE

Copyright © 2024 Nuerdias Huupkanse

All rights reserved.

INTRODUCTION

Ragdoll cats are among the most affectionate, laid-back, and strikingly beautiful breeds in the feline world. Their captivating blue eyes, luxurious coats, and endearing personalities make them an irresistible choice for many cat lovers. But bringing a Ragdoll cat into your life is more than just welcoming a furry companion; it's embarking on a rewarding journey filled with joy, responsibility, and commitment. This guide is designed to empower you with the knowledge and confidence needed to care for your Ragdoll cat and ensure a happy and fulfilling relationship.

From the moment you decide to welcome a Ragdoll cat into your home, preparation is key. Kittens, with their boundless curiosity and playful energy, bring excitement and occasional chaos. Preparing a safe and nurturing environment is the first step toward a harmonious coexistence. Kitten-proofing your home, creating a welcoming safe space, and understanding potential hazards are crucial for your new companion's safety and comfort.

The early days with your kitten will set the foundation for your future together. These are the moments when trust and bonds are formed. Understanding your kitten's needs and behaviors during this adjustment period will help ease their transition into your home. Socialization, positive reinforcement, and gentle handling are essential to fostering a well-adjusted and affectionate cat.

Caring for a Ragdoll cat involves more than just providing food and shelter. Their dietary needs require careful consideration, as a balanced diet supports their overall health and well-being. Selecting the right food, bowls, and even treats ensures they receive the proper nutrition while also making mealtime an engaging and enjoyable experience. Incorporating interactive toys and foraging games can stimulate their minds and promote their natural hunting instincts.

Every Ragdoll cat deserves a space that caters to their physical and mental needs. From scratching posts to cat trees and a variety of toys, creating an enriching environment is crucial. Encouraging positive scratching habits not only protects your furniture but also satisfies your cat's instinctive behaviors. A comfortable bed and cozy resting spots will complete their haven, providing them with a sense of security and relaxation.

Health care is a cornerstone of responsible pet ownership. Regular vet visits, vaccinations, and preventive measures against pests and worms are vital to keeping your Ragdoll cat healthy. Finding a trusted veterinarian and understanding the costs and benefits of cat health insurance are important steps in ensuring your pet receives the care they deserve. Emergencies can arise, and being prepared with knowledge and resources is essential for your cat's well-being.

Grooming and hygiene are particularly important for Ragdoll cats due to their luxurious coats and unique needs. Regular nail trimming, brushing, and occasional bathing help maintain their coat's luster and prevent matting. While declawing may seem like a solution to scratching issues for some, it's essential to explore humane alternatives and understand the potential health complications that declawing can cause.

Litter box maintenance is another critical aspect of cat care. Ragdoll cats, like all felines, can be particular about their litter box preferences. Factors such as the location, size, and cleanliness of the litter box play a significant role in ensuring they use it consistently. Investing in the right tools, such as high-quality litter scoops and odor-removal products, can simplify this daily task while keeping your home fresh and clean.

Dental care is an often-overlooked aspect of feline health but is particularly important for maintaining a Ragdoll's overall well-being. Regular teeth brushing and dental care routines can prevent issues like tartar buildup and gum disease. Starting dental hygiene practices early in your cat's life will help them adapt and ensure their oral health is maintained.

Ragdoll cats are not just pets; they are cherished family members. Their affectionate and loyal nature makes them unique, but it also means they thrive on attention, care, and love. This guide is a testament to the joy and fulfillment that comes with raising and caring for a Ragdoll cat. By understanding their specific needs and characteristics, you can build a lasting bond and provide them with the happy and healthy life they deserve.

Whether you're a first-time Ragdoll owner or an experienced cat parent, this journey is an opportunity to grow, learn, and share countless moments of joy. Each stage of your Ragdoll's life will bring its own challenges and rewards, but with preparation and dedication, you'll create a harmonious and fulfilling relationship with your feline companion. As you embark on this adventure, remember that every effort you make is a step toward a lifetime of love, trust, and companionship.

CONTENTS

Chapter 1: GETTING YOUR KITTEN SAFE-ROOM READY, KITTEN-PROOFING, AND OTHER THINGS.. 1

Chapter 2: FIRST DAYS WITH YOUR KITTEN AND THINGS TO WATCH OUT FOR.. 5

Exploring Your Home.. 9
Kids and Kittens.. 10
Kitten Safety in Your Home 11
Summary of Things to Watch Out For: 13
Socializing Your Kitten 14
Holding Your Kitten 14
Training your kitten for good behavior 16

Chapter 3: DIET, FOOD AND WATER BOWLS, TREATS 18

Food and Water Bowls 21
Treats... 23
Treats with Interactive Toys and Hunting Games........... 24

Homemade Foraging Toys 25

Chapter 7: SCRATCHERS, TREES, TOYS AND BEDS
.... 27
Choosing the right scratcher.. 29
Tips and Tricks to Promote Positive Scratching Habits .. 35
Put Your Scratcher in the Right Place 35
Cat Trees 36
Toys 39
Cat Wands 40
Undercover Mouse 41
Cat Tunnels 42
Catnip Toys... 44
Other kinds of toys.. 46
Boxes and Bags.. 47
Cat Beds 47

Chapter 5: VETS, CARRIERS, VACCINATIONS AND CAT HEALTH INSURANCE... 50
Choosing your veterinarian... 50

Emergency numbers 51

Cat carriers 52

Vaccinations, pest and worm treatments 56

Vet Costs 57

Cat Health Insurance 58

Choosing a pet insurance policy 60

Chapter 6: NAIL TRIMMING, DECLAWING AND GROOMING 62

Choosing your nail scissors 63

Why Do People Declaw? 65

Cat Health Problems That Arise from Declawing 66

Solutions BEFORE You Declaw 67

More Reading on Declawing 68

Grooming 68

Should you bathe your cat? 70

Chapter 7: LITTER BOXES, AUTOMATIC LITTER BOXES AND LITTER SCOOPS 72

Where should the litterbox go? 73

How many litter boxes do you need? 76

How big should the litterbox be? 77

How often should you clean the litterbox? 77

BEST Litter Scoop Ever 81

Stain and Odor Removal 82

Chapter 8: DENTAL CARE, TEETHING AND TEETH BRUSHING.. 84

Teeth Brushing 85

Maintaining a Healthy Ragdoll Cat 87

CONCLUSION.. 87

Chapter 1

GETTING YOUR KITTEN SAFE-ROOM READY, KITTEN-PROOFING, AND OTHER THINGS

Before your Ragdoll kitten comes home, you'll want to make sure that your house is ready for its newest member.

Start by setting up a room just for your kitten. This is where you'll bring your kitten when you come home for the first time. Make sure it is a peaceful, quiet place for your new baby.

A spare bedroom connected to a bathroom is a good idea, as you can put the food and litterbox into the ensuite (but never put them next to each other! Would you want to eat next to your toilet? Nope! And neither does your kitten.).

Your kitty needs their own dedicated room so that they can gradually adjust to the surprise of living with you. It will be a big shock to have moved from their babyhood home to yours!

The less stressful the introduction, the better the chances are for long-term happiness. A separate room means your kitten can get used to the sounds and smells of your home on their own terms. It will help him/her become comfortable enough so that they start to play, eat, go the bathroom and more.

Anticipate your kitty being in this room for around 1-2 weeks. The full length of time will depend not only on the individual kitty, but also on whether you already have resident kitties, dogs or other pets; as well as whether you have children (and how old they are), and how much time you spend at home.

So, what should you have in this room? At a minimum, this room needs to have:

- Food
- Water
- Litter box with litter
- Toys
- Scratchers
- Grooming essentials
- Carrier

You also need to kitten-proof your home. This is just what it sounds like – baby-proofing, but for kittens. Your kitten is a baby too, and they are curious and mischievous. You'll want to make sure you tie up or put away the following:

- Cords on blinds
- Electrical cords
- Poisonous plants – all lilies, amaryllis, English ivy, philodendrons, poinsettias
- Anti-freeze
- Cleaning supplies
- Rat killer/bait and other poisons
- Aspirin
- Tylenol
- Strings
- Needles
- Sewing supplies
- Christmas decorations - such as icicles and breakable baubles (and hooks)
- Yarn
- Coins

- Rubber bands and hair bands
- Balloons
- Cotton balls
- Plug-in air fresheners – read an article about how toxic plug-in air fresheners and other air fresheners are for kitties.
- Snowglobes – read an article about how a kitty died from a snowglobe that broke.

Take a good look at your home from your kitten's perspective. Believe me, it's a good idea to get down on the ground and look at things from a kitten's point of view.

Think of it as toddler-proofing. Look for small spaces that a kitten may hide or get stuck in. Move breakables to a safe place, check for loose cables and electric wires. If you have pull blinds on the windows, tie them up (I just made them high enough so that the kitties couldn't reach them) or you can get child-proof tubes at one of a home improvement store to put around them.

If your kitten is a "wire or cord" chewer you can protect your electric cords and computer cables - and your kitten- with the same plastic tube covers. Wall socket plug covers are cheap, easy to install, and will keep paws safe.

Keep string, yarn, thread or ribbons in a container or a drawer that your kitty cannot access.

Be sure to close all drawers and cabinets completely – kittens may jump into ajar drawers and get stuck behind them, or find dangerous items inside cabinets.

And remember - you don't have to live like this forever! This is just something for the kitten stage.

Be sure to check out the Bringing Your Ragdoll Kitten Home – Checklist at the end of the eBook. You can print it separately and bring it to the store with you.

Chapter 2

FIRST DAYS WITH YOUR KITTEN AND THINGS TO WATCH OUT FOR

While many Ragdoll kittens adapt to their new homes quite easily, some might take just a little bit more time to adjust to their new surroundings. You need to be patient and loving during this phase.

The first few days may be difficult for your Ragdoll baby; after all, your little kitty has been used to being with their mom, brothers and sisters in a family environment. Suddenly they are not there anymore – so your new kitten might cry and call for them.

Likewise, the sights, sounds and smells of your home might make for a few initial nervous days.

The best time to bring a new Ragdoll kitten into the household is when you are sure you can devote the time to helping your new baby adjust to this big change in their little life.

Make sure you can be off from work for a few days or more. Getting the kitten on a Friday means you have all weekend to acclimate this precious new member of your family.

Many readers have reported how glad they were that they took a week off work to be with their new addition. A week allows you to spend a lot of time together, to begin socialization and, if your kitten is friendly and ready for it, to introduce them to any close friends and relatives that visit your home often, so that they are cool and relaxed with newcomers and situations.

If you are getting your kitten shipped to you, your breeder will let you know about the particulars. More than likely you will pick up your kitten in the cargo area of your nearby airport.

If you are picking up your kitten, then you will need to check with the airlines to see what their requirements are as far as carriers, flights and restrictions. Some airlines only allow so many carry-on pets per flight; others may require the kitten to carry in the cargo hold. You also will need to pay additional fees.

The time your kitten needs to adjust to your home will depend entirely on the personality of the kitten.

When I brought Trigg home (November 8, 2009), he didn't want to get out of his carrier at all. I shouldn't have forced him to get out, but I did and he quickly found refuge under the bed - his "safe" room was the guest bedroom and my boyfriend at the time slept in there with him.

It took Trigg about 24 hours to feel comfortable enough to use his litterbox and start eating. This is not terribly uncommon, depending on stress of the trip and maturity of the cat/kitten. Once they eat and use their box, you know they are starting to settle in!

On the other hand, when I brought Charlie home (October 15, 2009), he burst out of his carrier and ran around the room (my bedroom); he played and then eventually decided to eat. This was just the first sign of his outgoing personality.

Despite his obvious curiosity and the fact that he felt comfortable very quickly, I did continue to keep Charlie confined to a room when I was out of the house, because kittens can get into things they shouldn't - and if I wasn't home, I wanted him to be safe.

Charlie's reaction was totally different than what I expected. I expected he would have the same kind of reaction as Trigg, because they had been in a carrier for 10 hours, they both flew on an airplane, were both walked around the airport, came home in a vehicle and then finally arrived at a place that didn't smell or look like their previous home.

Trigg's reaction was more what I was accustomed to and expecting, not the rambunctious and playful response from Charlie!

So I guess you never know what to expect. The most important thing is to be soft, gentle and sensitive with your new baby and allow them to show you what their personality is like.

Enjoy the learning process - I strongly believe that we are joined with certain souls in this life in order to learn and grow – just as they are with you to learn and grow too!

When you arrive home for the first time

When you get home with your kitten, go straight to their "safe" room and place the carrier (with the kitten inside it) on the floor. There should be no other animals or children inside this room.

Open the door of the carrier and let your new kitten come out when s/he is ready.

You might consider taking the door off the carrier; so that the kitten can come and go from this carrier as they please. Carrier doors sometimes close with gravity, so it can be wiser to take off the door altogether.

Don't worry about how long it takes your kitty to emerge. You've heard the expression "curiosity killed the cat", right? Spend time with your kitten in this room for the first few hours. Your kitten comes with built-in curiosity, so s/he will come out of the carrier in due time, when they are comfortable enough to explore the new surroundings.

Don't rush this process. If you can, get down on the floor to talk to your kitten, and to play with them once they emerge from the carrier. When you are down on their level it provides added security.

Once your kitty is out of the carrier, show them where the food and water bowls are. Introduce them to the litter box, but make sure this box is at least five feet away from the food and water. I usually take the kitten and put them directly into the litter box – so they understand it, feel it, etc.

If your "safe" room is a bedroom, all the better because then your kitten can sleep with a member of the family. This creates an excellent bond. Of course, don't plan on a ton of sleep, unless you are a heavy sleeper - Charlie liked to play a lot at 3am!

Try to set aside about 20-30 minutes before YOUR bedtime to play with your kitten. Happy kittens and cats hunt, eat, clean and sleep. Your goal is to provide the "hunt" and "eat" portion, so that you can sleep while they clean and sleep.

A [cat wand toy](#) or a [laser pointer for cats](#) will have them running, leaping, etc. around the room and is the most ideal exercise for playing/hunting before bed. When you are finished playing, put out a fresh can of food – that way, your kitten will crash after eating and be fast asleep by the time you fall asleep too. This will hopefully mean you will also have a longer night's sleep! Rinse and repeat for the next several nights until the kitten is used to your routine.

Before too long you'll need to go back to work after the weekend or your week off. When you leave the house, ensure your kitten is confined to their safe room with plenty of food and water so that they cannot harm themselves or get into mischief. There would be nothing worse than coming home to an injured kitten!

There is no need to rush the first few hours or days that the kitten is in your home. Spend a lot of time playing and bonding during the first week. Sometimes a kitten is ready to explore the new home within a few hours (i.e., [Charlie!](#)) and other times it will take longer.

If you are patient with your new kitten, the transition will be smooth!

Exploring Your Home

Depending on the confidence and curiosity of your kitten, you can start to socialize them with the rest of the family and your home as they become comfortable with their new surroundings.

After a few days, a week or two weeks, you can begin opening the door of the safe room. Let your kitty decide when to venture out and explore the rest of the home, and never force this process.

Always make sure your kitten can dash back into the safe room if they feel scared or have had enough exploring for one day. This safe room is "home base" – it needs to be accessible at all times.

Your kitten will start to explore your home, beginning to get to know their new family and surroundings. It helps to ensure this is fun for them. A string, cat wand toy, or another kind of cat toy is a great way to interact with your new kitten during this time and heck, any time!

If you have a resident kitty or other resident pets, then there are specific steps you should follow to ensure that introductions go well and everyone learns to get along. Check the specific sections towards the end of this guide for instructions on how to introduce your new kitten to your resident cat or dog.

Kids and Kittens

If you have young children, you will need to encourage them to be calm and quiet around the new kitten at all times. It's important that they refrain from making loud noises, screaming or squealing with excitement, and running or sudden movements.

Of course, this can be hard because your children are naturally excited and they want to interact with their new kitten!

Depending on the age of your children you will need to adjust your approach. If your children are very young, you will need to be present at all times to ensure the kitten is not frightened and that your kids don't do something wrong or dangerous without understanding their actions. Many a kitten has been loved to death from a cuddle that was too tight or went on too long.

If your children are older, you can help them understand how the kitten feels by reminding them of a time when they were scared or apprehensive themselves, and how they might have wanted to run or hide. Explain that this is how the kitten feels, and that it's important to let the kitten approach by itself. Never allow a child to force affection or attention on a frightened or unwilling kitten.

It is best if children can take a cool, calm, collected approach, as it helps to keep kitty from being startled by unfamiliar sounds. Think of it as introducing your children to an infant. Try this in small doses so that everyone has time to get used to each other and the kitten learns that they don't need to be frightened of your kids.

Soon the kitten and your children will be best of friends – your kitten might become your child's next doll, being dressed up in clothes and strolled around in a stroller like Rags was.

It's also important to teach children how to hold a Ragdoll. Ragdolls can be quite floppy, as their name implies! Children need to learn how to support kittens properly under their chest and rump. Let them know to put the kitty down carefully if s/he wants down.

Teach your children to leave a sleeping kitten alone as well, as this is when kittens grow and develop. Your kitten can be in deep sleep and shouldn't be disturbed. If your kitty is awakened a lot from much needed naps s/he may resort to sleeping where s/he won't be bothered as easily, like under beds or out of sight. Kittens sleep over 85 percent of each day when young, just like little human babies!

Kitten Safety in Your Home

Kittens and cats of all kinds like little hidey-holes all over the house. Keep this in mind as you are going about your daily activities in the home.

Remember to check lower cabinets, dishwashers, clothes washers and dryers before closing, just in case your kitten has decided it would be a nice place to hide, nap or play.

Keep doors to the dishwasher, the washing machine, the clothes dryer and the chest-type freezer closed at all times, except for when you are standing there. Never leave a door open, even for a moment as kittens are quick and can easily hide inside. You might not miss them at first and they could really get in trouble.

A suggestion about the clothes dryer: always stand by it a few moments after it is started and listen for any bumping. Better safe than sorry.

Trigg loved my clothes dryer when he first arrived – as seen in the photo. Especially because I have dryer balls that make fun sounds. However, I quickly discouraged his interest in the dryer by throwing the clothes from the washer quickly in the dryer – he didn't like being in the way!

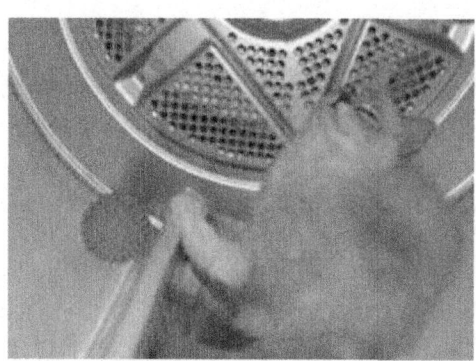

Let family and guests know that they should watch the small opening where door hinges are, and the front/outside of doors as they open and close them, to avoid little kitten paws and tails getting caught inside (Rags' tail always had a little crook at the end of it because it was shut in a door at one point).

Remind visitors that your kitten is an indoor pet, and should not be let outside. A break-away type of collar with a bell on can be a good idea so you know if your kitten is under-foot, as well as where s/he is when near doors. They can be very sneaky! Just make sure it is a "break-away" style so the kitten does not catch him/herself on something and choke.

Be careful when raising or lowering recliner chairs and power beds as kittens can often play underneath and can be hurt by the metal working parts.

Also, remember to check under quilts or throws on beds and couches before you sit down on them. Kitties like to burrow in a warm nest to sleep!

Common sense and caution will make your home a safe and loving environment for your new kitten.

Summary of Things to Watch Out For:

- Washing machines
- Clothes dryers
- Refrigerator or freezer doors
- Hot oven doors
- Hot stovetop burners (an empty burner that has just been turned off) - If your cat or kitten gets near the stovetop, a good suggestion is to keep a large tea kettle with water in it and place it on the still-hot burner until it has cooled off.
- Recliners and/or recliner-rockers
- Unprotected screens in windows

Socializing Your Kitten

Socialize your kitten by handling it often – but gently! This is even more important for a kitten that is not-so-confident.

You can encourage visitors to hold, play and touch your kitten, so that your new cat gets used to strangers and how other people might interact with them. This also helps them adapt to change.

No matter where you are in life – just out of college, an empty nester or about to have children – helping to socialize your kitten for your lifestyle will make your life easier in the long run.

Touch your kitten everywhere! They should be used to you touching their paws, face, legs, tail, belly, you name it. One of the great benefits of getting a cat from the kitten stage is that you can "train" it to accept being touched by you and anyone else anywhere on its body.

This makes for much easier vet visits in the future and your vet will thank you.

Holding Your Kitten

When it comes to handling your kitten, you want to hold them so that you don't scrunch any of their limbs. My cousin was sweet enough to send me photos of her holding her sweetie Huck, so that you can see the various styles.

When walking around with a kitten in your arms, it's best to do like they do at the cat shows. They run their hand up underneath the cat from back to front, with the weight of the cat weighing mostly on their forearm and open palm underneath the chest/ ribs. Their legs are actually on each side of your forearm.

I've seen many folks walk around with their kitties being carried that way while they are doing other things with their other hand/arm. It's amazing to watch. I made this video on YouTube about how my sister and I hold Ragdoll cats (which will come in time after the kitten stage).

Vets sometimes do this too. By holding the cat this way, the entire length of the cat's body is supported. Of course, when Ragdolls get to be 15 to 20 pounds or more, it's much harder carrying them around.

You might want to pick up kittens by gently supporting underneath their rib cage with one hand and cupping your other hand around their rump. As you get them up close to your body or your chest, move that hand to support their backs while still holding them by their rumps. It's much like holding a baby when burping them.

I also like to hold my cats like a baby in both arms, with their belly up. Some kittens come already doing this, whereas others have to learn to trust you holding them that way. Many Ragdolls love the belly-up thing, but there are many that do NOT. Those are the ones you carry with their undersides supported on your lower arm or else in the burping position.

Keep in mind that every cat is different, and you just want to make sure that you hold them so that they are always comfortable and supported.

What it boils down to is that if your kitten is comfortable – that is, not squirming in your arms or complaining about being there – then you are doing it right. See more photos of how to hold a cat and how to hold a kitten on the site.

Training your kitten for good behavior

If there is a behavior in your kitten that you do not like, you might redirect its attention by moving it somewhere else and rewarding the new behavior. Never spank your kitten!

A common problem is when kitty jumps up somewhere you don't want them to go – like on your countertops, the dining table or the stovetop. An easy way to deter that behavior is to use a product like QuitIt that makes a hissing type of sound and scares the kitty from doing it again. They will soon learn that they need to avoid counters/tables in order to avoid such noises.

Another inexpensive option is a simple sound deterrent. Just put 20 pennies in an aluminum drink can and then tape the opening closed so they don't fall out (the Miller Lite Aluminum Cans with screw tops are PERFECT for this).

When you see your kitten doing something you disapprove of —just shake the can with the pennies. Kittens and cats do not like that sound! The sound of the pennies on the aluminum will really discourage them from continuing their misbehavior.

If you have potted plants that your kitten will not avoid, consider buying decorative bark or rock that will not interest them as much as that loose, rich soil. You can also put aluminum foil over the dirt, as they don't care for the feel of the aluminum under their paws.

Chapter 3

DIET, FOOD AND WATER BOWLS, TREATS

Food recommendations, such as what to feed your kitty and when, should come from your breeder and then ultimately from your vet.

Decisions about food and diet are something that you will have to make based on your budget, your lifestyle, your living situation and your vet recommendations (and whether or not you trust your vet or if you think s/he is being paid by the large pet food companies to sell products). You might find this page on our site helpful.

There is a great cat resource online written by a Californian veterinarian, Lisa A. Pierson, DVM, that addresses the dangers of a dry food diet.

Keep in mind that the recommended food quantities on pet food containers are based on the amount needed by active cats living in multiple cat households. The amount needed by sedentary, neutered or spayed cats is often much lower.

Remember that cats in the wild eat many small meals per day and providing smaller meals more frequently might help your kitten avoid problems with obesity later on.

Be sure to monitor eating habits in the first week. You'll want to at the very least continue the food regime that the breeder recommends (based on what the kitten was eating while s/he was at the breeder) until your kitten is comfortable in your home. If you intend to switch their food, you have to do it slowly to prevent stress and diarrhea.

Make sure you start by using the food your breeder was using. Your little kitten will already be stressed out in a new environment and not as inclined to eat. The smell of the food they ate at their breeder's home will be familiar, and it will encourage them to eat.

If you decide to feed your kitten a different brand, ensure you take it slowly. Gradually mix it up to 50/50 with your kitten's previous brand, over the course of about a week, before switching entirely over to the new brand. This way, your kitten's body will adapt to a different diet.

Be sure the brand you switch to has low or no by-products and is high in protein for the best health of your kitten, especially in the first year of growth.

If you have a multiple cat household, you might eventually consider setting up several feeding stations throughout your home – that way cats can avoid or greet the cats they want to without fighting and more importantly, without spraying!

It will totally depend on your situation though; these days Charlie and Trigg have one feeding station in the kitchen and they eat peacefully next to one another.

However, we didn't start out that way – they both growled at each other (and me!) when they ate. Much like a puppy, you have to make a point to socialize your kittens around food. If you have kids, this is doubly important as kids are less predictable and don't realize that a pet they know and love can turn on them.

You can feed treats by hand when your kitten first comes home at 12 weeks. Hand feed, stroke him/her while s/he eats and remove (or refill, as is more often the case) their food dishes WHILE s/he is eating from them.

Your vet will ultimately appreciate your efforts around your cat's mouth. They'll need to do oral exams, so the more comfortable your kitty is with its mouth being touched by human hands, the better.

Your kitten will also thank you. At some point in the future they'll need to take pills for one reason or another, and it's good if they're already used to you hand-feeding them and touching their mouth gently.

Food and Water Bowls

There are a lot of options when it comes to food and water bowls for kitties.

Plastic food bowls tends to hold bacteria and are also known to cause feline acne. I do like <u>ModaPet bowls</u> that are made from plastic – Charlie does not get acne from everyday use of these, but Trigg does get <u>feline acne</u>. However, I have found that Trigg doesn't get acne if I only feed one meal a day in those bowls – so that's what we do!

So you may want to choose a heavy glass bowl, a metal bowl or a ceramic bowl instead. Be sure that it is dishwasher-safe to make your life easier.

A water bowl is essential for your kitten, especially if you choose to only feed your kitten dry food. You will want to get something sturdy and deep, like a [PawNosh Cubby Bowl](). Some kittens like to play in the water and if it's sturdy, then they cannot tip it over, so it's less clean-up for you.

You might consider having at least two water bowls in different areas, especially if you have a two-story home. That way, if one is spilled, your kitten has access to another and won't go thirsty.

If your kitty is on an all wet food diet, you will be surprised to learn how little water they drink. In fact, Charlie and Trigg don't even have a water bowl, because they never drink water. But remember, all cats are different so you should start by offering water!

You can learn more about how wet food gives cats the moisture that they need in their diet when you read [Dr. Lisa Pierson's Cat Info Site]().

If you do have a water dish, you might consider dropping a few cubes of ice into their water bowl every day. Many cats love playing with the ice until it melts (make certain the kitty is there at the bowl when you drop in the ice cubes). Then, when they are done playing, you can refill the water bowl(s) with fresh water.

Moreover, when kittens are teething, cold things always seem to help little gums as the teeth are coming in. The trick really is for them to get the chips into their mouths. You want to make sure you are there for safety's sake - never leave the area until the ice chips/cubes are completely melted.

Another option for water drinking is to get a [cat water fountain]().

I prefer to use individual bowls because that works for us – but there are different products on the market depending on what you're looking for. Check out the "Shop " portion on the site, where I feature bowls and food that we've reviewed for ideas of what may work for you.

Treats

I only recommend a few treats. These are Whole Life Pet cat treats (which can also be fed to dogs), Honest Kitchen's Wishes as well as Eden Foods' Bonito Flakes.

The Whole Life Pet Products' cat treats are freeze dried versions of the muscle of an animal – so for example, their chicken treats are literally freeze-dried chicken breast – pure and simple and natural. They also have an Organic treat line.

Read our reviews and see our video review here (we have reviewed a lot of flavors – so just click on each link of the flavor you're interested in).

Honest Kitchen's Wishes are freeze dried, 100% human-grade, wild caught Icelandic Haddock. These come in giant pieces that can be broken into smaller bits, but can be eaten as a whole piece – and the challenge of eating the big piece is a good exercise for your kitty. Available in 2 oz. Read our review and see our video review here.

Eden Foods' Bonito Flakes are shaved Bonito flakes that are tested as safe for human consumption. You can buy bonito flakes at major pet retailers, but those ones are usually not tested for human consumption – mercury and other nuclear levels in fish are something to be aware of! Read our review and see our video review here.

Treats with Interactive Toys and Hunting Games

I love, love, love interactive toys because they decrease mental stagnation and prevent behavior problems which result from boredom in your cat.

They also bring out the instincts your cat has to hunt for their food. The Nina Ottosson's Interactive treat puzzles are excellent for this.

We have tried out the Dog Spinny and the Dog Brick Game. There are different levels, so you want to start with level one, which in our case was the Dog Spinny.

These games are made from plastic. I prefer the plastic ones because they are dishwasher-safe and easily cleaned. Again, you need to watch your kitty and make sure s/he is not developing feline acne as a reaction to the plastic.

Homemade Foraging Toys

If you're a crafter or you would prefer not to spend money on toys, you can make safe homemade foraging toys too.

One homemade toy is to use a plastic beverage bottle – make sure you have run it through the dishwasher and make sure to clean the cap too (you could also use an empty plastic peanut butter container).

Cut holes in the sides of the bottle that are large enough for the treats to fall through, then stick the treats into the bottle and screw on the lid. When you put it on the floor, your kitty will start knocking it around trying to figure out how to get to the treats (that is, of course, if they like the treats you put inside).

A foraging toy such as this one can keep cats entertained for hours. It's ideal if you are gone all day because it will keep your kitty busy until you return.

You can also make homemade puzzle feeders where you cut a hole in a cardboard box and the cat has to paw their food out of the box. Cat Amazing is a product that does this for you – you can see a video of how it works here.

You might even want to hide food or treats in different places throughout your house so that your kitten has to "hunt" for his or her food while you're at work.

My vet suggests throwing their treats across the room so that they get exercise chasing after them!

Chapter 4

SCRATCHERS, TREES, TOYS AND BEDS

Starting your kitten out with the right scratchers, toys and beds will hopefully avoid destruction of your furniture for years to come.

Cats aren't vindictive. They don't set out to scratch furniture or drapes because they are cross at you or they want to cost you money; they do it because they have an instinct to scratch.

Scratching is a marking behavior. There are special glands on a cat's paw that release their scent. When they scratch, they deposit that scent on the thing they're scratching — and consequently it becomes an area they want to return to: think, "MINE!"

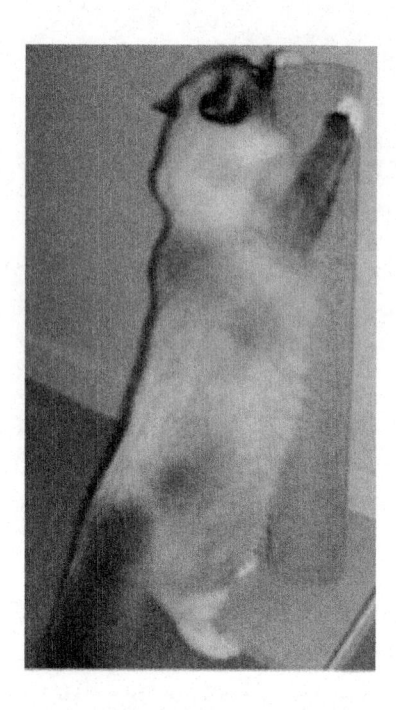

When you start out with a kitten, rather than an older cat that has established scratching habits, you can teach your kitten where it is OK to scratch.

So, for example, when Charlie, as a kitten, would go for the corner of my bed skirt as a great place to scratch, I would say, "No!" and then pick him up and take him over to his [Bergan Turbo Scratcher](#) and put him on that for scratching.

The great thing about the Bergan Turbo Scratcher is that the corrugated cardboard portion is replaceable so you can remove it, flip it over to get the use out of the other side and then [order replacements](#).

Now, at 8 years of age, he goes to that Bergan Turbo Scratcher and scratches away! The Bergan Turbo Scratcher also makes for a phenomenal toy that your kitty will play with for the rest of its life. See Charlie playing with his Bergan Turbo Track at 2.5 years old!

In other words, the way that I trained Charlie to use the Turbo Scratcher (or corrugated cardboard) instead of my bed skirt was by rewarding him with praise (I use a high-pitched voice to praise) and giving him pets when he did what I wanted. I do not believe in punishing, swatting, slapping or hitting your cat – I simply redirected the undesired behavior he was displaying. Such a tactic is non-violent and will make your kitty love you all the more.

Choosing the right scratcher

Most cats prefer to scratch either horizontally or vertically; they also usually have a preferred scratching material.

Since your kitten is learning what s/he likes, you will want to provide variety. If your kitty favors one over the other after you've tested a variety of scratchers, you can always donate the ones they don't like to a local animal shelter. You may find that your kitty likes to use a range though, as mine do.

I suggest starting with both an upright scratcher, such as TopCat Products' Sisal Scratching Posts or Natural Sisal Cat Tall Scratching Post from Felix Katnip Tree Company.

You can also choose a horizontal scratcher such as the PetFusion Ultimate Cat Scratcher Lounge - it's a bed and scratcher in one – or the Felix Katnip Tree Company Scratching Beam.

I DO NOT suggest choosing ANY scratcher for your cat that has carpet on it. Allowing your cat to use a scratcher covered in carpet will only encourage your kitty to scratch carpet that might be on your stairs or in a room, which can be quite costly to replace. Even if you don't have carpet in your apartment or home right now, you might move and that could change in 10 years, so it's better to be safe than sorry.

You want your kitty to know that carpet is off limits; therefore it's best to choose scratchers that use cardboard or sisal.

Read our reviews on these products to help your decision:

- TopCat Products' Scratching Post Review
- Natural Sisal Cat Tall Scratching Post from Felix Katnip Tree Company Product Review
- PetFusion Cat Scratcher Lounge Product Review
- Felix Katnip Tree Company Scratching Beam Review

The Felix Katnip Tree Company's Tall Scratching post is tall and big enough that it could easily double as a cat tree for a small kitten – so you can see if your cat is a climber and likes to be up high.

My Charlie likes to be high up, whereas Trigg is more of a ground dweller. And a tall scratching post with a platform on top will help you determine if a cat tree would be a good purchase for your kitten in the future.

Here is our review video of the Felix Katnip Tree Company's Tall Scratching Post.

Many scratchers come with catnip that you can sprinkle into the corrugated cardboard or that you can rub on the sisal post, to attract your kitty to the scratcher and encourage them to use it.

However, most kittens usually can't smell catnip until they are over six months old, so while the catnip approach works well for an adult cat, it will have no effect on your little baby!

Instead, you can use toys like the Neko Flies or strings to encourage your cat to check out the scratcher. This is what we did with Charlie and Trigg to encourage them to use and explore the TopCat Sisal Posts.

I just took the Neko Flies cat wand and hovered it over the top of the post. They wanted to get to it so much that they would just climb the pole without realizing!

When you combine play with a scratcher, it becomes a great two-in-one toy for a kitten. It's also a technique you can use to introduce them to new scratchers

Another scratcher and cat bed that I cannot get Trigg off is the Petstages Snuggle Scratch and Rest. It's made of corrugated cardboard and shaped like a bowl, so it's easy for a cat to feel cozy in it! You can see more of Trigg enjoying his scratcher in this video.

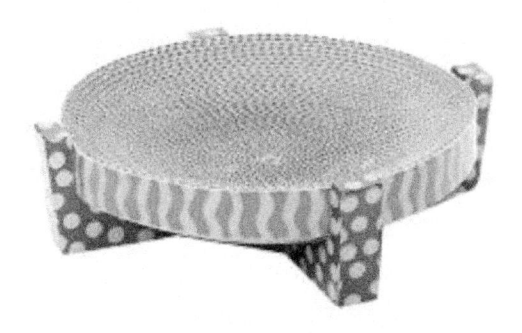

Another great scratcher that also doubles as a bed is The Original Scratch Lounge - Worlds Best Cat Scratcher.

All the cats in our family have loved these lounges. The Original Scratch Lounge is a three-sided scratcher with a reversible floor – the older kitties like to rub their face against the corners of this scratcher.

Another great scratcher is the kittyblock. It is a cube made of corrugated cardboard that has a square cut-out in the center, so they can go on top or inside.

Check out this photo of Charlie on one – you can tell it is a nice size. Here is our arrival video of the kittyblock which will show you more of it and you can see how the cats interact with it.

Whatever scratchers you decide to buy, be sure that they are sturdy (cats are easily discouraged from a non-sturdy object) and are made of materials such as cardboard, natural wood or sisal rope.

All the scratchers I have mentioned above also have replacement options – so in other words, when your kitty has used the scratcher to the point where it needs replacing – you can buy a replacement pad or pole or just another one from any of these companies.

Tips and Tricks to Promote Positive Scratching Habits

Offer the right scratching options – a vertical scratcher and a horizontal scratcher – and preferably two different materials like a sisal scratcher and a cardboard scratcher. That way you can figure out which direction your kitty like to scratch and also which type of material your kitty prefers.

Two-in-One Scratchers – Since scratching releases emotions and also used as a way to stretch after a good nap, it's a bonus when a scratcher doubles as a bed as well, like the PetFusion Ultimate Cat Scratcher Lounge.

Deterrents – Products like "Sticky Paws" work well to deter your kitty from scratching on the corner of your couch. You put it on the corners of your furniture and anywhere else your kitten may want to scratch. It's basically sophisticated double tape and cats hate that sticky feeling on their feet. Aluminum tin foil also works well, as they tend not to like the feeling of that on their claws.

There's no reason to think or expect that your kitten will be destructive, as long as you provide for his or her needs.

Put Your Scratcher in the Right Place

It is important to place the scratcher close to where your kitty wants to scratch – this can be next to a window, near a sleeping area or another favorite area. When Charlie was a kitten, I noticed that he always liked to scratch when he woke up from a nap, so I typically had a scratcher close to where he slept.

Believe me, once their scent is on that scratcher, they will not care where you move it – they will find it and use it. For example, Charlie's Turbo Scratcher used to be in the master bedroom, but since I got sick of hearing the ball roll around the Turbo Scratcher at 3am, I moved it to the guest bedroom and that's where he uses it now.

Now that he is older, he also doesn't play at 3am anymore, so when we have house guests, I simply move the scratcher back in my room and he always knows where it is! Now he plays at 6am!

Also, to discourage 3am play on the Turbo Scratcher, simply turn it upside down and slide it underneath a dresser or a sofa for the night. Just remember to turn it upright early the next morning or else your kitty will go searching for it.

Cat Trees

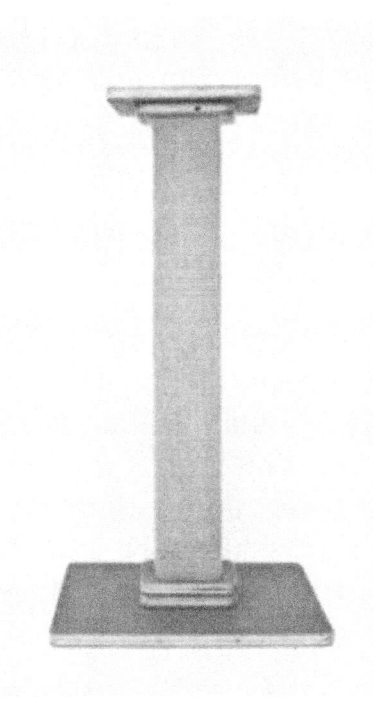

A question I'm often asked is what kind of cat tree I recommend.

I have a page on the site where you can see some of the great cool cat trees on the market. And we always have great discussions on our Facebook page about such things.

As a rule of thumb, most cats like to be able to get up high and survey the world from a safe perch. Sometimes they might settle in on top of the cabinets or bookshelf, or find another spot in your house. But remember, it all depends on the cat – some prefer to stay closer to the ground and a cat tree can become an expensive dust collector.

As I suggested in an earlier chapter, I think it's wise to first start out with a tall scratching post like the Felix Katnip Tree Company tall scratching post because it has a ledge on the top. If your kitten is attracted to scratching on the post and climbing to the top, then I would say s/he is a candidate for a cat tree.

We never had a cat tree for my Rags growing up, and it was never a problem to be without it. He had plenty of beds, desks and more that he made into his domain.

When it comes to a cat tree for a Ragdoll cat, you want to worry less about the height and focus more on the size of the base. The reason? Sturdiness – think of a cat running full speed and launching onto the tree. You don't want it rocking and banging against the wall or falling over and hurting something. Aim for a base of around 4 feet as this provides good stability. If you have a handy person in the family, you could even have your tree of choice mounted onto a new, wider base.

If you want to guarantee that the tree doesn't rock, put up an anchor point and tether the tree to the wall.

Here are some suggestions Ragdoll owners on our site have given for cat trees:

1. Costco sometimes has great sturdy cat trees
2. Armarkat Cat Trees
3. Molly and Friends Cat Trees
4. You&Me Cat Trees
5. DIY Tree. Most of the plans I've seen online for giant trees are free. Even if the materials cost you $500, at least you know exactly what it's made of and can build it to accommodate what your cats likes (tunnels, ramps, perches, hammocks).
6. Catification. This book by Kate Benjamin and Jackson Galaxy has a plethora of ideas and examples of what

people do to provide alternative cat tree ideas inside a home.

We have reviewed a cat tree that we love, but it is no longer on the market. Here is a link to our review of that product, in the case that you are a DIY-er and want to make this one yourself.

When I do cover cat trees on the website, all the reviews and mentions are covered here.

Toys

Toys play an important part in the bonding process between you and your new kitten, and they have an important role in overall kitten health and well-being. An enriched environment for your kitty provides them with increased activity, a decrease in mental stagnation and it can end up preventing many kinds of maladaptive behavioral problems.

Remember rule #1! Your hands and feet are not toys!

Do not allow or encourage your kitten to bite your hands, feet, fingers or toes. Use a toy instead. When we first got Charlie, we played with Charlie with our fingers and when I brought Charlie to the vet a few days later, he went after the vet's fingers because that's what we'd accidentally taught him to do!

It was so embarrassing, especially when she said, "I see someone has been playing with Charlie with their fingers!" Here's a popular video on YouTube of us being guilty of that.

Instead, here are some great toys to consider buying for your new kitten that s/he will also enjoy as an adult cat.

Cat Wands

Cat Wands are a great first toy option for your Ragdoll kitten, and well-made ones can provide a tremendous amount of exercise.

There are two varieties of cat wand toys that I have really come to like - Neko Flies and the Bird Catcher Pro wand toys. Both remind me of fly fishing.

Ellen is the owner and creator of Neko Flies, and she invented these products as she was sick and tired of cat wand toys that easily fall apart – and believe me, we have gotten our fair share of products to test that have done exactly that!

So when I recommend these, I do so whole-heartedly. They have been a hit with Caymus, Murphy, Charlie and Trigg as well as the two domestic short hairs belonging to a friend of mine. And it is an instantaneous love.

You can buy the wand and attachments separately, so that your kitten regularly has a new attachment to play with.

After raving about Neko Flies for years, I was introduced to the Bird Catcher Pro Ex, which is now my new favorite cat wand. It has an extendable interactive cat teaser wand rod (more like a fishing rod) with guinea fowl feather refills and storage bag.

I cannot stress how much I love the easy storage of this one! It's so nice that it reduces in size so that it takes up less space and tucks away easily. You can see our review video of the Bird Catcher Pro Ex here. It really provides awesome entertainment and exercise.

Another wand toy that is quite popular and supported heavily by Jackson Galaxy, host of Animal Planet's My Cat from Hell, is Da Bird. I have never used it, but have heard great things about it, so you may like to try that too.

Undercover Mouse

My aunt adopted a Ragdoll named Prince William from Sweden. Prince William was sent the Undercover Mouse toy by one of her friends, and Prince William would play with it for hours.

As the name of the product suggests, there is an undercover "mouse" that moves around under a nylon skirt. This interactive cat toy brings out the hunter/predator skills in your kitty – just watch the videos on our YouTube channel to see how Charlie and Trigg got into it.

Unfortunately, this toy is no longer made under the Undercover Mouse name but there are now several on the market that are similar:

- Petlink Mystery Motion Concealed Electronic Cat Toy
- SmartyKat Hot Pursuit Cat Toy
- Cat's Meow Cat Toy

So now I know five Ragdoll cats who love this thing! It also has various attachments that you can buy afterwards to keep the stimulation varied.

Cat Tunnels

Cats love to hide in cozy spots, and so a cat tunnel can be a great way of providing a safe haven right in the middle of the lounge room.

The Petstages Cuddle Coil is a polka-dot popup play tunnel that you can usually find at any large pet store or online. Kitties love the protection and comfort that it provides. It's made of cuddly-soft padded nylon material that encases a sturdy coil for comfort and support. The back is enclosed for added security and privacy.

I don't know what it is about the Petstages Cuddle Coil but it seems that every cat likes these – at least, every cat that I have seen interact with it!

Caymus (pictured here) is eight years old and he still plays in the tunnel my mom got him as a kitten! He definitely sticks out the back end, but he loves it – it totally puts him in a good mood and makes him a purring machine. Here's a video of Caymus playing in it.

The Cuddle Coil might be on its way out – but we have reviewed other cat tunnels too.

- Pets Can Play Ultimate Cat Tunnel Product Review – this is a large tunnel, great for a large breed cat like a Ragdoll cat. Might be "huge" for a kitten, but certainly will grow into it.
- SmartyKat Crackle Chute Cat Toy Collapsible Tunnel – this is a VERY popular cat tunnel for kittens. It makes a crinkly sound that excites kittens.

Catnip Toys

Did you know? A cat's reaction to catnip is genetic! About 15% of cats don't have the gene so they are immune to catnip's effects. But all kittens, whether they have the gene or not, don't develop a sensitivity to catnip until they are 6-9 months old. So just ask your breeder if your kitten's parents respond to catnip to know whether your kitten will too.

Once your kitten has grown enough to develop sensitivity to catnip, you can start offering them this wonderful treat.

Hands down, my favorite cat toy of all time is the Yeowww! Catnip Banana!. It is shaped like a banana – the outside is a yellow canvas- like material and the banana is stuffed with 100% pure organic catnip. It will last for years and 99% of the time your cat will love it and play with it daily.

My mom first discovered these when Rags was 15 years old and she put one in his stocking at Christmas. It was a hit thereafter. Rags never played with toys past the first 15 minutes, because after that cats become immune to the catnip "effect" for at least a few hours. But the Yeowww! Catnip Banana was a toy that he returned to over and over again.

You might want to buy one to test how your kitty responds to it – and if they love it, you can move onto buying them in bulk as I do now. Every time a friend gets a kitten or their cat has a birthday, they get a Yeowww! Catnip Banana from me.

Watch a video compilation of Caymus, Murphy, Rags, Charlie and Trigg all playing with Yeowww! Catnip Toys.

You'll want to find out what the breeder has been using for toys and see what she or he suggests for your new kitty. Your kitten will be used to these toys and your breeder can tell you which toys your kitty likes best. If she doesn't know their names, have her send you a photo to see if you can find them at the local pet store.

If you have dogs or small children that might eat cat toys, avoid the toys that have plastic centers - they are small, can be dangerous to ingest and are a child choking hazard. If you have little children, be sure all toys for your kitty are child-safe too. For example, it might be a good idea to have cat toys that are all the cloth type (like the Yeowww! Catnip Banana).

If you choose a stuffed toy and your kitty pulls the stuffing out, throw away the toy immediately so your kitty doesn't eat the stuffing. This is one of the reasons I like the Yeowww! Catnip Banana, as it doesn't have any polyfil – just 100% pure catnip.

Other kinds of toys

There are so many different toys you can choose for your Ragdoll.

Crunchy foil/mylar balls are popular with kittens. My mom's 13-year-old, Murphy, still enjoys them quite a bit – he hauls them around the house in his mouth, meowing while he walks. Of course, you can make something similar just by wadding up a sheet of foil paper into a ball.

Felted wool is a material that is traditionally safe for kitties, and it has a smell that many kitties like. Many Etsy sellers make fancy felted wool balls like these or you can also grab wool dryer balls from Amazon.

I bought wool dryer balls for my clothes dryer and accidentally pulled one of them out of the dryer with my clean clothes. It made its way upstairs with the clothes and the next thing I knew Trigg was batting it around on the floor.

Great free toys include bottle caps from plastic bottles – I like to throw them across the room and the cats love to chase them and bat at them. These could be a choking hazard for a small child or a dog, though, so be careful.

Another cheap toy you can make is to take two or three cable ties (these can be purchased in bright, vivid colors) and loop them together like a paper chain. Remember to snip off the pointed ends. These toys go scooting across the floor and the cats love them. They can also be carried around in their mouths and taken to another area for play. Just remember to make the loops large enough that they cannot swallow them.

You can get these ties in 13 - 14 inch lengths at any home improvement store, often in a bag of 100. They're cheap entertainment for both kittens and older cats alike – and heck, you might already have these in your home. Easy cat toy!

I also make this homemade toy with a wire dry cleaner hanger and the end of a check book. Here is a video of Charlie and Trigg playing with the toy.

Boxes and Bags

Kittens and cats love to play in boxes and paper bags. Boxes provide a sense of security and cats love to hop in and out of them. You can turn a box upside down and cut a hole out for them to enter and peek out of.

When it comes to bags, make sure the bags aren't plastic, as these can be suffocation hazards for your kitten. The brown paper ones from the grocery store are best because they usually don't have handles. Handles can wrap around a kitten's neck and if they cannot get out of it, they can be strangled to death – especially if they are not being supervised.

Cat Beds

A cat bed is another item you might want to get for your new kitty. Often a kitten will like to sleep on the couch or a chair – like Charlie and Trigg – but those items might be off limits in your household. In that case, a cat bed is a great option.

Cat beds don't have to be expensive. You can make one out of an empty box with a small towel in the bottom (which is easily removed for cleaning).

You can also buy a round cat bed. Kitties love to sleep in round beds. I recommend the Alpha Pooch Siesta Bowl – it comes in a brown color and is natural.

As far as soft and cozy beds, we have also liked the Urban Paw beds. I have included links to our reviews below. Also, places to buy with discount codes are also there:

- Urban Paw Luna Orthocomfort Cuddler Cat Bed in Sherpa Fuschia Product Review
- Urban Paw Jumbo Milo 2-in-1 Designer Cat Bed Product Review

Some of the scratchers I've already mentioned in this guide also serve as cat beds – Petstages Snuggle Scratch and Rest and the PetFusion Cat Scratcher Lounge.

Chapter 5

VETS, CARRIERS, VACCINATIONS AND CAT HEALTH INSURANCE

Choosing your veterinarian

If this is your first cat and you don't yet have a vet, then you will want to get a recommendation. Ask a neighbor, a friend or a family member– and be sure this person takes the same kind of care of their animals as you intend to take care of yours.

You can also look for local vets online and research their reviews on their own business Facebook pages, for example, or on Yelp or other such review sites. There are regular vets, specialty vets and holistic vets practicing in all areas.

You can also make an appointment to just talk with your new vet. Have a list of questions on hand, so that you can ask the vet and get a good feeling (or not) about whether this is the right vet and clinic for you.

If you know the date that you will be bringing your new kitty home; you should go ahead and schedule a vet appointment for that day or soon after. For example, I got Charlie on a Thursday, and he met my vet the next day. I got Trigg on a Saturday and he met the vet on Monday (and Charlie didn't meet Trigg until Trigg had been cleared by the vet – of course, they came from the same cattery, but you can never be too sure and I didn't want to jeopardize either one of them).

Emergency numbers

Once you have chosen a vet, phone or visit to ask questions such as whether walk-ins are permitted or if appointments are always needed. Ask about emergency clinics and services, and take down the emergency phone number straight away – put that in your phone immediately and keep a copy on the fridge or next to your home phone. It's best to be prepared because you never know when an emergency may occur.

Once you know what the emergency procedures are, make sure you have easy and quick access to their phone number.

My mom has one of those label makers, and she used it to type out the emergency vet's name and number in case there is ever an emergency with any of her animals. She put the label on every phone in the kitchen and then at strategic phones throughout her home. I know the number by heart but since there are so many people in and out of my parents' home, she wanted it everywhere, especially if she was out of town.

You also want to find out the Animal Poison Control Center's number for your country. Inthe United States it is (888) 426-4435.

They are the best resource for any animal poison - related emergency, 24 hours a day, 365 days a year. Be aware that as of August 2017, a $65 consultation fee may be applied to your credit card. Some microchip companies offer free, 24/7 ASPCA - certified veterinary consults with a subscription (i.e. Home Again), and some pet insurance companies, like Nationwide, also offer a free 24-hour vet line.

Cat carriers

The reason I included "carriers" with the vet visit here is because it is very important to bring your kitty to the vet in a carrier. As much as you might want to hold that little bundle of fur during the trip, it's not safe.

If you are travelling by car or public transport, your kitten needs to be restrained. If there is an accident or something happens to scare your kitten, a cat carrier is the best way of keeping them safe. In a car, your kitty can become a projectile if you have to stop suddenly!

Your kitty needs to be protected during the trip, and while you are entering the vet clinic; so that they can't leap out of your arms into the parking lot or onto a busy street.

Moreover, when a kitty gets scared they can sometimes have a reaction you won't expect and they can injure you by trying to get out of your arms. This is especially true at the vet, which will have smells, sounds and sights that your kitty isn't used to, not to mention other strange cats in the waiting area and scary dogs too!

Reducing your young kitten's exposure to other cats will decrease their stress as well as their exposure to illness, which is another reason to have a great carrier.

The proper pet carrier gives your kitty the safe haven they need. You can take steps to ensure the carrier smells like your home, by keeping it inside and in the kitten's room, so that they can go in and out of the carrier as they like.

This means your kitten will start to see the carrier as a snug place for a nap rather than something to be scared of because it only comes out when a vet visit is on the cards. Your kitty will associate it with love and protection!

If your kitten is being shipped to you when they first arrive, the breeder will have them in a carrier that you pick up from the airport – and you will have already paid for the cost of the carrier and the shipping charges of the cat.

If you've done your research and you already have a preferred carrier in mind, you could certainly ask your breeder if you can ship one to them, so that your kitty comes home in the carrier you want. If you do this, the carrier will have to meet strict airline regulations.

If you go to pick up your kitten from the breeder in person, then you will need to take a carrier with you. Be sure to get a carrier that your kitten can grow into to save you money in the long run – you'll want one that is large enough for a 25 lb. animal.

I like any carrier that allows you to take off the top – in other words, one like the Sleepypod or most of the Petmate Pet Carriers (I like their Kennel Cab Fashion Carrier) will work for this purpose. It's useful because the vet can unscrew the top of the carrier (or in the Sleepypod's case unzip the top) and have full access to the kitty. The Sleepypod has a weight limit of 15 lbs, though – so just be aware that your kitten will probably grow out of it.

The Sleepypod and Sleepypod Air are the only pet carriers that have been truly tested for pet safety in a vehicle crash. So they are the safest carriers on the market. We have reviewed them both – the only issue with them is their size restrictions. The Sleepypod Air is specifically designed for air travel, but can be used in your vehicle as well.

- Sleepypod Air Review on Floppycats
- Sleepypod Review on Floppycats

Long ago, my mom purchased two of the Marchioro Cayman Clipper carriers. To this day, they remain my favorite carriers for transporting kittens in a vehicle.

Here is a review video of the carriers. My mom has had them for 13 years, and they are still going strong.

Many people keep their cat carrier in an area where the kitten or cat can use it as an alternate bed (this is the idea behind the Sleepypod – when not used as a carrier, it is a stylish bed and looks like a fancy round bed when the top is zipped off).

To make a plastic carrier into a bed, remove the door and keep a towel or soft padding inside and it will become a place for naps and play. This will make the carrier a less stressful place to be when the kitten is transported to and from the vet.

Vaccinations, pest and worm treatments

Breeders usually do the first round of vaccines for your kitten and this is based on the breeder's opinion on what vaccines are necessary. Some breeders administer the vaccines themselves where others havethem administered by a vet.

It's likely that your breeder will have already ensured your kitten has received their first round of shots, and they'll tell you when the next ones are due.

Your breeder will probably include a health record for your kitten, and this should show the stickers from the vaccines your kitten has received. The stickers are important because they show the brand, lot number and expiration date of the vaccines.

In choosing which vaccines, flea treatments and worm treatments your kitten/cat should receive, you will need to know the benefits and risks of both. This is not something I can recommend or not recommend. It is a personal decision based on your lifestyle, your beliefs and where you live.

You'll want to get a full understanding from your vet as to the benefits and side effects of the vaccines. A well-respected holistic veterinarian, Jean Hofve, has an excellent website that addresses a lot of cat health related questions called, Little Big Cat. She also has a page on vaccinations in cats and the dangers involved in the over-vaccination of kitties which might give you more insight and help you in your decisions about vaccinations.

Dr. Jean and I also had a telephone interview about vaccinations that you might enjoy listening to or reading for additional information.

More than likely your vet will have a recommended kitten vaccination schedule. There might be vaccinations required within the city/county/state where you live as well. Your vet will know this information.

There's always a chance that your kitty could get sick or could come to you sick, so it's important to be aware of these symptoms of a sick cat, which include:

- decrease in appetite
- diarrhea
- vomiting
- dull hair coat
- listlessness
- weight loss
- red, watery eyes
- sneezing
- nasal discharge
- straining when urinating or defecating
- frequent trips to the litter box
- bloody urine
- changes in litter box habits

Vet Costs

Vet costs can vary enormously. I checked with my vet, KC Cat Clinic in Kansas City, MO, USA for these figures, which are current as of August 2017. Obviously, these will be different depending on where you live. Also, please be aware that KC Cat Clinic's prices include a lot of doctor time talking about lifestyles and behavior things to look out for – this isn't only about vaccinating kittens.

1st year vet costs will be around $600 for a healthy kitten. This does not include Feline Leukemia vaccinations, FIV testing, spaying or neutering. Many breeders will only send you your kitten when it has already been spayed or neutered. I prefer breeders that do this, because it shows their responsibility in keeping the breed strong.

KC Cat Clinic spaces out their vaccines over the 16-week period recommended by American Association of Feline Practitioners. Of course, if they see something they are concerned about, like a skin issue, then the cost for the first year can obviously change.

You definitely want to check anticipated costs with your own vet – and even check yourself with KC Cat Clinic if you are in the Kansas City area and planning to use them.

Cat Health Insurance

Depending on where you live, you may be interested in getting cat health insurance. There's no way to know what might happen to your kitten during its lifetime.

Many of my readers have health insurance for their pets and I know it is offered in many countries outside the USA.

If you're familiar with my site, then you know that my Rags was diagnosed with lymphoma at the age of 16 and had to go through chemotherapy treatments and what not. We did not have cat health insurance and therefore, it was a very expensive endeavor.

Because of this and because there are limitations to cat health insurance policies in certain areas, you might consider setting aside the amount you would normally pay for a premium and setting up an additional bank account just for your cat.

KC Cat Clinic recommends putting aside $50/month per cat in a separate savings or money market account. That way if anything happens in their life time, you can use the money from that account. If your cat remains healthy, then you've got a great savings account set up.

Of course, you have to resist the temptation to dip into it for other purchases! That's when health insurance can prove a better option.

After my parents' dog, Napa, had cancer, I decided to get pet insurance for Charlie and Trigg when they were six years old. I chose the whole pet with wellness plan from Nationwide. I like this plan because it covers more than just emergency vet visits, and it also covers dental, unlike some other plans. It was an excellent decision for us.

If you decide to get a quote from them, please do let them know that Jenny Dean with Floppycats sent you.

Addie, my sister's Ragdoll has an ongoing illness - Feline Gastrointestinal Eosinophilic Sclerosing Fibroplasia. Luckily, when my sister adopted Addie as a rehomed Ragdoll, Addie's previous owner had signed her up for pet insurance through Healthy Paws. I say, luckily, because the discovery of Addie's disease cost $10,000 – she would have lost her life without the emergency surgery she needed and the follow-up medical stuff.

Addie's policy had a $250 deductible and 90% reimbursement rate, and my sister paid around $22 per month for the policy. It covered emergency surgeries, hospital stays, ultrasounds, blood tests, etc. Addie also needs regular ultrasounds, which Healthy Paws continues to cover.

At the end of it all, my sister ended up owing about $1,000 instead of the full $10,000 because of her insurance. Healthy Paws does not offer a plan like the one I have for Charlie and Trigg – they cover more emergency surgery type of stuff.

Choosing a pet insurance policy

So, how do you know which company and policy is right for you? It's important to get quotes first from different insurance companies. In the United States, rates are determined based on:

1. Breed of cat
2. Pet's birth date
3. The state you live in

I simply made a chart listing out all the insurance companies that my vet suggested. Then I CALLED each one (I did do some of the online quotes) and found out:

1. Monthly fee for insurance
2. Annual deductible amount – they are usually $100, $250 or $500
3. Reimbursement level – you can usually choose from 70-90%
4. What the plan covered – if it was more than just accidents, illnesses and chronic illnesses.

Since I got pet insurance when Charlie and Trigg were already 6 years old, I could reference their old vet bills. I added those bills up over a year. Then I totaled the monthly fees plus my deductible –

and when I discovered I could potentially break even from having health insurance, I took out a plan.

You can find reviews online of different health insurance policies – it's always wise to ask your vet about it because they usually have had direct contact with an insurance company through other clients. They can share that client's experience – for example, my vet put me on to Nationwide because other clients had reported how much they liked them. And the vet liked working with them too. The vet didn't get a cut for recommending them either, so I knew I was safe with the recommendation.

I still phoned about six other companies though. It was a full day ordeal to figure out what I wanted to do, and the monthly fee would have been cheaper if I had signed them up as kittens.

My premiums will probably change over time as the monthly fee is not always set in stone, but right now I pay $46.48/mo per cat or $557.76/year plus the $100 deductible I have - and our plan covers 90%.

So, when Trigg had a dental procedure shortly after I signed up for it, the cost from the vet was around $700. After paying the $100 deductible, Nationwide reimbursed me $540 from my claim.

My sister also works for a company that offers pet insurance as one of their benefits! So, you might check with your HR department and see if there's an option for pet insurance coverage.

To find pet insurance companies in your country, simply Google "pet insurance" or "pet insurance Australia", for example. A reader told me this website was helpful for her in deciding on which pet insurance to get.

Chapter 6

NAIL TRIMMING, DECLAWING AND GROOMING

It's important to trim your cat's nails from a young age. I have heard so many stories of people who cannot clip their cat's nails and therefore have to haul them to the vet to have it done. It's best to get them used to it as a kitten, so that it's an easy process for the remainder of their life.

Trimming your kitten's nails is an important part of the bonding process, not to mention an important part in making sure your skin isn't accidentally clawed when they are sitting on your lap and kneading. Sharp nails can hurt – even when your kitten doesn't mean to use them intentionally!

To get your kitten used to nail grooming, handle their paws often when you are grooming and petting them. Make sure to spread their toes and push on their pads lightly, so they get used to the feel of you touching their feet.

If your kitty is not happy or compliant, try doing just one foot at a time. Give extra love and a snack afterwards, to help this become a more positive experience. It will get easier in time.

Some kitties have ticklish back feet, so be patient. When I started trimming Charlie and Trigg's nails, I usually tried to catch them right after a nap so that they were still sort of sleepy and not nearly as responsive as they would have been right before playing.

Cats have five nails/claws in the front, including the dewclaw, and usually only four in the back.

The part of the nail that you want to trim is only the tiny sharp white tips. Never trim back to the pink quick! This pink section has a blood supply and your cat will feel pain and bleed – just as you do if you accidentally rip a nail off at the quick.

Front claws will probably need trimming every three to four weeks. Back feet may only need to be trimmed every two or more months or so, as they usually wear differently than the front feet – back claws don't get the same scratching workout that front claws do.

Trimming your kitten's claws from the beginning will help your cat gets used to the feeling of you extending their claws out to cut them, as well as the safe compression of the scissor cutting down on their claws.

If you have the chance to watch me trimming my cats' claws in the video links below, then you can tell that neither one of mine are really fazed by this harmless process.

Choosing your nail scissors

It's best to use a scissor that is especially made for kitties (like the ones pictured below). They have a shape that's different to normal human nail scissors and it will be more comfortable for your cat.

The JW Pet Company GripSoft Nail Clipper for Pets, Small work just fine.

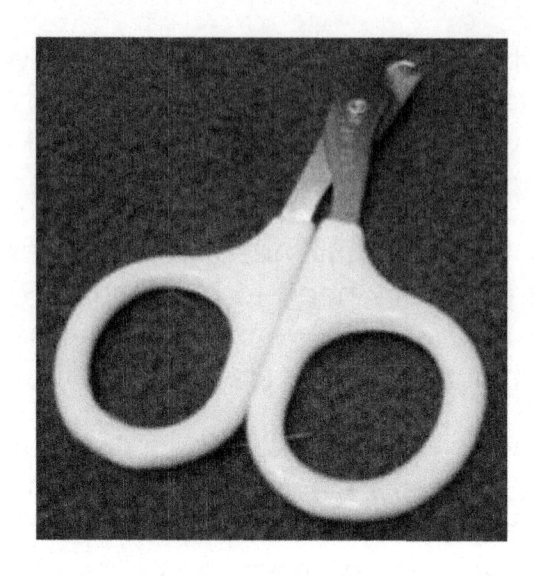

I have also reviewed the Zen Clipper, and they are my current favorite. The link to my Zen Clipper review will also take you to a video of how I trim my cat's claws.

To learn how to trim your kitten's nails properly, have the vet show you on your first visit.

You can also see the video I made when I trimmed Trigg's nails with the JW Pet Company GripSoft Nail Clipper for Pets, Small.

You might also enjoy this video of my sister trimming her cats' claws – she has a different approach because her cats were not used to their nails being trimmed when she first got them as re-homed Ragdolls. My sister uses the Whisker Wishes Veterinarian Grade Pet Clippers in that video. She still uses them and likes them just fine.

Declawing

This section on declawing was not a part of my original book.

As an American, I am ashamed that we still allow this horrible practice in our country. Declawing has been illegal in other first world countries for so long that many readers don't know what Americans are talking about when we say the word, "declaw"!

Declawing is not just removing the claws from your cat's paws. It is an invasive surgery that removes the entire last bone in your cat's toes as well. Think of it as being the same as removing the top joints of all of your fingers.

The surgery is usually performed on the two front paws; however, some cat owners choose to have the back paws done as well.

When I first learned that fact, it made me realize how behind the times we are with such a barbaric practice. And since this book is sold and read all over the world, I hesitated to include it because I didn't want it to even be a consideration for your new baby.

But in the years since the first version of this book was published, I have been asked enough about declawing that I have decided I need to include this section for those who are not aware of its harmful effects.

Why Do People Declaw?

Declawing is a decision that some pet owners make for their own convenience. It is never a decision made in the best interests of the feline.

Sadly, the reason most owners declaw their cats is just to avoid the cat scratching and destroying their furniture. This is a tragedy, as responsible cat ownership shows that cats can easily be trained to stay away from furniture and use their special scratchers instead.

Other people declaw their cats because they don't want to themselves or their children to be scratched, when this is really a minor issue that rarely happens.

I believe that if people really understood the crippling effects of cat declawing, they would think twice about doing it and hopefully choose not to do it altogether.

Heck, one Google image search of a bad cat declaw will make your stomach turn. Declawing can lead to lifelong problems for your kitty.

Cat Health Problems That Arise from Declawing

As with any surgery and post-surgery procedures, there are health issues that can arise from declawing your cat. Infection is a key one.

Another common problem is that a cat will stop using the litterbox because their paws hurt and the litter makes them hurt more. So, while you didn't start out with a cat who peed outside the litterbox, you might get one after the fact.

More importantly, a cat uses its claws to release emotions as it scratches. Think about it – your cat will usually scratch when they are excited to see you or when you come home, or after a satisfying nap or a lovely dinner. By taking away the tools that help them release such emotions – their claws – you also take away their ability to fully release their emotions in a positive way. This means they have to find other ways of releasing their emotions, like peeing or pooping outside the litterbox.

Claws are also essential for a cat to be able to stretch their front body muscles. If they don't have claws to dig into a scratcher and stretch their muscles, then the muscles will not perform in the capacity they were designed to. It can lead to many problems including early arthritis.

Solutions BEFORE You Declaw

As the primary reason many Americans declaw their cats is to avoid them scratching on furniture, you need to provide other scratching solutions in your home. Check the scratcher reviews in the earlier chapter to learn more about these.

Cats are attracted to their own scent, and scratching marks an object with their scent over and over again. If your cat has started to mark their scent on carpet or a piece of furniture, the best thing to do is to remove that piece of carpet or fabric. You can put it onto a cat scratching post to encourage them to use that instead. Or, try the avoidance techniques such as double-sided tape or aluminum foil that are also discussed in the earlier chapter.

If you are considering removing your cat's claws, I urge you to please read through all the links to information below BEFORE you make a decision about declawing your cat.

Declawing.com - **Learn about the harmful effects of declawing**

As I mentioned above, there are solutions to dealing with the scratching before you remove your cat's claws. The most important one is keeping your cat's nails trimmed (discussed in a future chapter).

A company called, "Soft Claws" makes a product where you literally superglue small plastic nail covers over your cat's nails. They are very fun because they come in a variety of colors, from black to pink. They also come in a variety of sizes--from kitten to large (for those of us with Ragdoll or Maine Coon cats). Soft Claws for Cats - Medium Black

More Reading on Declawing

There is a wonderful project called The Paw Project that has a plethora of information about declawing – and the humane alternatives to declawing. You can watch this excellent film they put together.

Here is some additional reading on our website about the subject:

- Declawing Cats Alternatives, Problems, and More from a Ragdoll Rescue Expert
- Declawing Cats: Problems, Alternatives, and More

I hope in my lifetime that declawing is outlawed in the USA, just as it has been in other first-world countries around the globe.

Grooming

Most Ragdolls do not have fur that tangles and it is relatively mat-free. Their coats are usually medium to long and have a soft, silky texture. If you live in an area where there are four seasons, then your Ragdoll may shed more fur in the spring, for example, as they molt their winter coat for a lighter summer one.

Brushing is a great way to ensure your cat's coat stays in top condition at all times.

When Rags got old, he stopped taking care of his coat. Because he stopped grooming as often, he got mats. Thank goodness I got him when I was a little girl and he was used to being brushed with every doll brush I ever owned. This made it easy to care for him and brush his coat in his old age.

So it's a good idea to regularly brush or comb your kitten. Once a week is fine, but so is every day if they will accept it. Brushing not only helps to keep their coat soft and clean, it also creates a great bonding experience between you and your cat.

Brushing also helps your cat get used to being touched everywhere on their body (but beware the sensitive tummy area – you might get a scratch if your kitty is protective of it!) which is fantastic for future vet visits. It also helps you get to know your kitty's body so that you can watch out for scratches, injuries or unusual lumps or bumps in the future.

As far as which brush to get, ask your breeder what s/he has used. Charlie and Trigg hate being brushed, so they only like the Rakom Cat Grooming Tool and the Tangle Teezer – which is a human brush I found at CVS.

I keep a page on cat brushes updated on the site, with reader comments and more, so that you can figure out which one would work best for you. Or, you can get brush and comb recommendations from friends with long-haired cats, your vet or your breeder.

Cat Brush and Comb – What Are Your Favorite Cat Grooming Tools?

Some Ragdoll owners like to invest in complete grooming systems – especially if you are showing your animals. If this is the case for you, I recommend Scaredy Cut.

Scaredy Cut is a silent and vibration free trimming system that uses high quality barber scissors regulated by attachment guide combs.

A set of six guide combs provide regulated cutting from 0.5 inches up to 1.0 inches.

Scissor blades are guarded by the attached combs while cutting and the scissor tip is rounded for safety. You can use the Scaredy Cut scissor with the comb attached, to gently brush your pet prior to trimming.

Should you bathe your cat?

Overall, Ragdolls keep themselves clean and well-groomed.

In general, I do not believe in bathing cats (of course, if you are planning on showing your Ragdoll kitten that's an entirely different situation). I just don't think it's necessary if they are healthy and on the proper diet, etc.

And when you think of shampoo for cats, one thing always comes to my mind - how much they clean themselves! They lick every part of their body.

NEVER use a human shampoo on your cat. If you really need to bathe your cat, you must use a special shampoo and be especially conscious of rinsing it out well.

If for some reason your kitten needs a bath – say, to clean a dirty bottom or something along those lines - then I'd suggest using a shampoo like the Earthbath All Natural Hypo-Allergenic and Fragrance-Free Shampoo.

The Earthbath shampoo is 100% bio-degradable, cruelty free, soap-free, safe, gentle and effective, according to many readers!

Chapter 7

LITTER BOXES, AUTOMATIC LITTER BOXESAND LITTER SCOOPS

One great benefit of buying a kitten from a breeder is that your kitten's mama will have taught her babies how to use a litter box.

When you get your kitten home, make sure you start out by using the same litter your kitten has been used to using at the breeder's home. This will ensure the minimum of accidents as your kitten will be familiar with the feel and smell of this litter brand.

You can then move over to another kind of litter based on your vet's recommendation or, if you already have other cats, to what you're already using in your household.

Following this easy guide to make a gradual switch:

- Week 1: use 100% breeder litter in the box
- Week 2: add half of your preferred brand litter to make a 50-50 mix.
- Week 3: Increase your preferred brand to 75%.
- Week 4: Now use 100% of your preferred litter brand.

Where should the litterbox go?

To begin with, the litter box will be placed in your kitten's "safe room" from the start. If the "safe room" has a bathroom, that's a great place to put it.

I used to grab an old bath mat and stick it under the litter box, so that when the cats get out of the litter box it collects any bits that come off their paws. It's also easier to clean.

Now I rely on the WooPet! Cat Litter mats to do the job for me – I just love them. The loose litter falls into the holes of the mat and then I can dump it back into the litterbox to be used again. It does a much better job than the bathmats ever did.

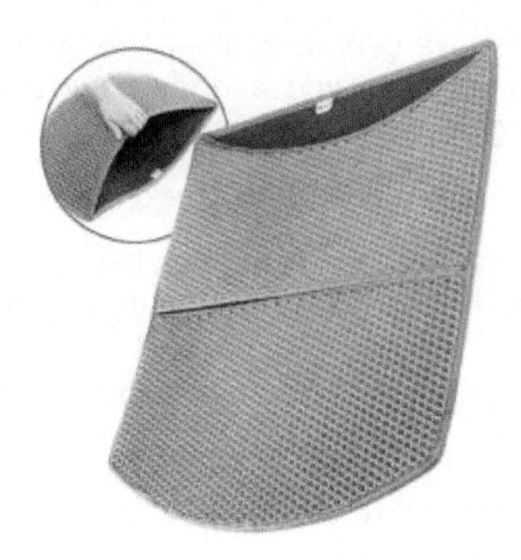

Readers love them too – we did a review video that shows how they work.

If you want a similar one that is much bigger, the Blackhole Cat Litter Mat is a great one, too, and here's our review video for that one.

You don't want to move your kitten's litter box around frequently. They need to get used to where it is, so that if they get discombobulated in your house, they will always know where to find the box.

Of course, if you are a one cat household or if you have two new kittens, for example, you can always have an additional litter box outside the safe room.

For example, when I brought Charlie home, his safe room was in my master bedroom/bath. I got sick of the litter box being in my master bath, so I put another in the guest bath and after a few weeks I removed the one in the master bath and Charlie used the one in the guest bath instead. Now if guests come, I just move it to the master bath until they leave... Trigg and Charlie have yet to have an accident – knock on wood!

I've read that a laundry room, bathroom or a den are great places for a litter box. My mom used to have her litter boxes in the basement (this isn't great if you are an out-of-sight-out-of-mind type of person because you can forget that they need to be scooped!). But it worked for my mom, because she had two German Shepherds and dogs are notorious for eating poop out of the litter box!

My mom had a carpenter cut out a panel in her 8 panel doors that the cats can use as a cat door. You literally don't even know there's a cat door there! You can see Napa in the photo below – she knows where the door is because the cats go in and out of it, but she cannot get through the panel! Here's a video of my mom's cat door.

With a good litter box habit, cats are probably one of the easiest animals to take care of because they do not demand a lot of attention and they can go potty indoors.

How many litter boxes do you need?

I once heard you should have one litter box, per floor, per cat. In my house, that would be six litter boxes! In general, it's usually 1 box per cat plus 1.

It really depends on how big your home is – one person's first floor can be much larger than another's. So try and think about your cat based on your square footage.

We used to have just three boxes, but over time, because of the amount of reviews we do, I have increased our number of boxes to five. I still think we would be fine with three – I had one in my master bathroom and two in the basement. I got used to a lot of litter boxes when Rags was going through renal failure (when you have an old cat in renal failure you scoop a lot because they pee a lot) and as a result Trigg and Charlie benefited from my constant cleaning of the litter box.

How big should the litterbox be?

Because a Ragdoll cat is a large breed cat, it's smart to have a larger litter box. You will need a larger litter box like this one or you could even get a cement mixing tub from a home improvement store. A lot of Ragdoll breeders do this.

The cement mixing tubs are designed for easy mixing and scooping, so they have a curved bottom and no sharp corners inside — which makes them perfect for scooping litter easily. They come in different sizes, the small tubs are around 24" x 20" x 6" and cost $6 or $7 and the large tubs measure 24" x 36" x 8" and only cost about $13.

Most commercial litter boxes aren't big enough for large cats, and they don't make any hooded boxes that are even close to being large enough. Another good substitute is storage boxes, like ones made by Sterlite or Rubbermaid that you can buy at Wal-mart or Target. Now that Charlie and Trigg are full grown cats, we have moved to storage bins for litter boxes – you can see a video of that here. I spent $5 per storage container.

If you have a hooded litter box, the ammonia odor is trapped in these pans and can really be offensive to your cat (and you!).

How often should you clean the litterbox?

A cat on a proper diet of moisture-rich canned food will often pee AT LEAST 3 x/day. That means that one cat with one box will have AT LEAST 21 urinations in that box before you clean his litter box at the end of one week. Therefore, it is recommended to scoop AT LEAST daily if not twice daily.

There should be NO ODOR present in a litter box. Use clumping litter so that all urine and feces can be removed and there will not be an issue with odor.

Clumping litter makes this easy. I only use clumping litter as all of the non-clumping litters are very unsanitary (in my opinion) and cause elimination issues. Non-clumping litter allows cats to walk in a litter box that is literally saturated in urine (dry or wet). When urine dries, things are made worse. The only thing that evaporated urine leaves is uric acid/ammonia after the water evaporates. This makes things worse because the uric acid/ammonia is highly concentrated.

If the litter does not clump, it's also harder to remove, and it will also leave remnants in the box. Plastic is porous, so urine soaks into it, leaving a lasting odor for the life of that box. You can use litter liners but the cost adds up over the life of the cat, not to mention the additional plastic that you are throwing away into the environment. Litter liners annoy many cats and really are not necessary if a litter pan is properly maintained.

As nearly all my litter boxes are near a human toilet, I tend to scoop them as often as I pee – I literally pee and scoop! It makes it easy, and keeps it clean. Cats are very fastidious, so it's important to keep your kitty's litter box as clean as possible. Think about it – would you want to walk on your old pee or feces to go the bathroom again? EW and YUCK! No one likes a dirty toilet. Cleaning the litterbox twice a day is the way to go.

Once a month you should dump the entire contents of the litter box and replace it completely. Clean it out with soap and water once a month – I watch it closely and when it gets "nasty" I clean it entirely. It's really up to you – if the litter has a lot of little clumps and smells then you need to change it more often.

If you use a disinfectant to wash the litter box, be sure it is safe for your kitty. Disinfectants that contain phenols and cresols can be lethal to cats as they can absorb them through their paws. Cats are also very allergic to Pine Sol and Antifreeze. My vet suggests 10% vinegar to 90% water.

I once [interviewed Dr. Elsey of Precious Cat Litters](#), who told me that plastic litter boxes should be completely replaced every year because they absorb the odors of the urine and feces. While you might not be able to smell it, your kitty can and such odors can discourage them from using the litter box. Buy a completely new box each year for your kitty! Again, I suggest reading more on Dr. Pierson's website - [Dr. Pierson's Litter Box Page](#).

Automatic Litter Boxes

When I first wrote this book, back in 2010, I did not know much about automatic litter boxes. Since then I have learned more as readers have enquired about them and told me about their experiences.

In November 2015, we were asked to review the Litter Robot Open Air and boy, am I glad we did!

The Litter Robot Open Air is an automatic litter box that is very sophisticated. It has a self-adjusting weight sensor that knows when your cat is inside using it (so you don't have to worry about it cycling when your kitty is inside of the litter box).

After each use, a timer counts down until it cycles, which is great because it allows the kitty to be way finished with their business before it cycles. It is also good for clumping litter, so that the clump has time to set.

The sifting system cycles automatically and dumps the clumps and waste into a drawer below. Once the drawer is full of waste, an indicator light lets you know that it's time to empty it. Someone was thinking when they designed this puppy. It's made in the USA and comes with a 90-day money-back guarantee and 18-month warranty.

Our review video is lengthy, but gives you a good idea if it would be a good fit for your household.

Another reader wrote a review on Floppycats about her experience with her two Ragdoll kittens and the Litter Robot Open Air.

The Litter Robot Open Air has been and continues to be a huge hit with readers. My sister recently reviewed it as well.

BEST Litter Scoop Ever

If you don't go the automatic litter box route, or if you do, you still might want to know about the best litter scoop ever.

I know it seems ridiculous that I would recommend a litter scoop, but seriously there is only one that I will ever use in my home and I have extras just in case! It's the Litter Lifter.

I have loved it for over 10 years – I've reviewed many others and this one still always wins. The Litter Lifter has peaked blades that allow loose litter to fall back into the box.

The scooper has a large surface area and it's efficient, allowing for less time and dust when cleaning the litter box(es).

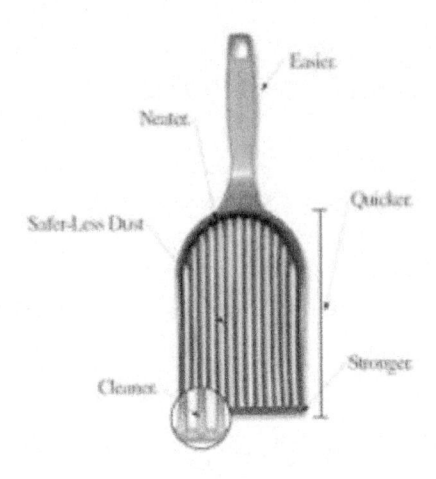

You can see what I mean by watching this video that features Charlie and Trigg!

Stain and Odor Removal

Accidents happen. Especially when you're a little kitty! You can clean your kitten with a wet paper towel or towel. Or just give them a bath with a pet safe shampoo.

I am not a fan of any "wipes" or "dry shampoo" stuff for cats – those things leave a residue that is not washed off like a shampoo. And ultimately, that residue has to be licked off by your poor kitty. Can you imagine having to lick off a soap-like residue from your skin? Yuck.

However, what about your carpets and upholstery? If you live in an apartment, then you may be even more concerned about cleaning up after your kitty.

We product-tested Fizzion years ago and it's still a staple in my house; you can see our review here and see the video of me product testing it.

Many readers have purchased Fizzion because of our review and also because of our mention of it in this book. They report how wonderful it is – even using it on their own clothes before throwing them in the washing machine.

Other readers have reported great things about Zero Odor too.

Chapter 8

DENTAL CARE, TEETHING AND TEETH BRUSHING

B ecause of the email concerns I have received about kittens who bite, I have chosen to add a section on "teething" to this guide.

Just like small children, kittens cutting their teeth need to release pain, and they do that by biting. Most kittens start losing their baby teeth at three months old and get a full set by nine months old.

You can look into their mouths to see if your kitten is teething. You can see the photo of Trigg's teeth below - for a week or so, Trigg had two canine teeth, because his adult tooth was growing in and pushing his baby teeth out.

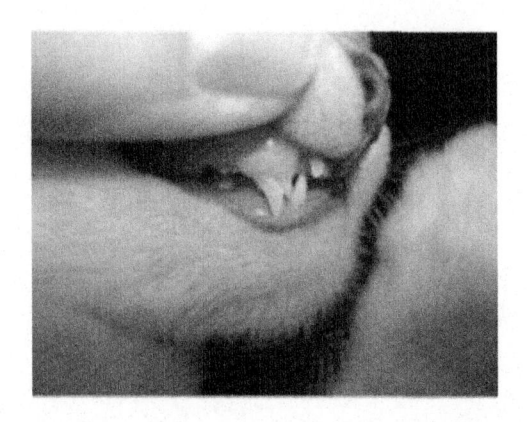

To help prevent your kitten using your hands as a place to release their pain, it is best to give her or him a soft toy s/he can bite down on - the Yeowww! Catnip Banana comes to mind - or ask your vet for a recommendation based on his or her experience.

Biting can be an issue separate from teething – but be sure to check their mouth first to see. We have an ongoing discussion on the site about biting issues in adult cats, which you can reference here, if needed: Ragdoll Cat Biting Problem.

Whenever my two little ones bit me (it is normal cat behavior between cats to bite one another – so they don't do it to spite a human), I would pick them up by their neck, like their mom would - look into their eyes and say, "NO!" and put them back down and ignore them. Paying further attention to them rewards the bad biting behavior.

Teeth Brushing

It's important to start your kitten's dental regime early. Cat dental procedures can cost hundreds of dollars and sometimes thousands, depending on what needs to be done. It is best to start them early to get them used to this process.

Cats in the wild catch mice or birds, and when they use their teeth to shear off heads and wings, the action cleans their teeth.

But a cat that is fed a commercial diet of dry or canned wet food doesn't have this advantage. Housecats are prone to gingivitis, holes in their teeth and even tartar. Contrary to popular belief, dry food is not necessarily better for cats' teeth (please read catinfo.org to learn more).

The best time to start the teeth cleaning process is when your kitten has their adult teeth in – starting from around six to seven months of age. Of course, it won't hurt to start opening your cat's mouth and rubbing their gums before then. They will get used to you touching their mouth and teeth. Be sure your hands are clean when you're doing it though!!

Because a cat's tongue is pretty effective in cleaning the inside of the teeth, you will want to focus on the outside. The worst patterns of disease seem to occur along the outside gum line.

Never use human toothpaste to brush your cat's teeth. It has fluoride and other additives that a cat should never ingest. I use [CET Poultry Toothpaste](#) – it's a poultry flavored enzymatic toothpaste for use with cats as part of an essential program for the pet's oral health. Cats do not have the ability to spit out food or their toothpaste, so it's safer to give them something they can safely swallow.

Here is [a video I took of brushing my parents' cat's Caymus' teeth](#) and another of [brushing Charlie and Trigg's teeth](#). You can also read more about [how to do brush your cat's teeth](#).

Of course, since you will see your vet shortly after your kitten comes home, it is a good idea to have your vet or a vet tech show you how to do this before starting it on your own.

You want to try and clean your cat's teeth twice a week, though a daily routine would be even better. You want to brush about 30 second per side.

CONCLUSION

Caring for a Ragdoll cat is a journey that enriches your life in countless ways. These affectionate and loyal companions bring joy, comfort, and unique moments of connection, making them more than just pets—they become cherished family members. To ensure a fulfilling and harmonious relationship, understanding their specific needs and characteristics is essential. This guide has provided a thorough exploration of what it takes to nurture and care for a Ragdoll cat, equipping you with the knowledge to meet their needs and enhance your shared life.

The foundation of any successful relationship with a Ragdoll cat begins with preparation. Creating a safe and welcoming environment sets the stage for a smooth transition, especially for a young kitten. By kitten-proofing your home and providing designated spaces for exploration and rest, you build a setting where your cat can thrive. These early days are crucial for forming trust and establishing a routine that benefits both you and your feline friend.

Nutrition and health play a pivotal role in a Ragdoll's overall well-being. From selecting high-quality food to incorporating interactive feeding methods, proper nutrition is key to maintaining their energy levels and promoting longevity. Regular veterinary care, vaccinations, and grooming routines ensure your cat remains healthy and comfortable, while also addressing specific needs related to their breed's luxurious coat and calm demeanor.

Ragdoll cats are known for their playful and inquisitive nature, making environmental enrichment a critical aspect of their care. Scratching posts, cat trees, and an array of toys not only provide physical stimulation but also engage their minds and prevent boredom. A comfortable bed and designated rest areas offer the relaxation they crave, completing their ideal living space.

Behavioral training and socialization further enhance your relationship with your cat. Gentle handling, positive reinforcement, and interactive play strengthen the bond between you and your Ragdoll, ensuring they grow into a confident and affectionate companion. Their unique personality thrives on attention and love, and your commitment to understanding their behaviors and preferences will only deepen the connection you share.

Maintaining a clean and comfortable home environment is another aspect of providing exceptional care. Proper litter box hygiene, stain and odor management, and solutions to common challenges such as litter box aversion help create a space that's welcoming for both your cat and household members. Dental care, though often overlooked, is equally important and can significantly impact your cat's quality of life.

Beyond the practical aspects, caring for a Ragdoll cat is an opportunity for personal growth and shared happiness. These gentle and loving creatures teach patience, empathy, and the value of companionship. They are uniquely attuned to their owners' emotions, offering comfort during difficult times and joy in moments of celebration. By dedicating yourself to their care, you experience the profound rewards of their loyalty and affection.

As you navigate the stages of your Ragdoll's life, from playful kittenhood to serene adulthood, you'll face challenges and celebrate milestones. Each step along this journey is a chance to deepen your understanding of their needs and strengthen the bond you share. Whether it's mastering grooming techniques, refining their diet, or addressing unexpected health concerns, your commitment to their care ensures a happy and fulfilling life for your feline companion.

Ragdoll cats remind us of the beauty of unconditional love and the simple joys found in daily interactions. The journey of caring for them is as much about the small moments—the gentle purrs, the playful antics, and the quiet companionship—as it is about the big achievements. In return for your care and devotion, your Ragdoll will offer you a lifetime of trust, loyalty, and joy.

In closing, the relationship you build with your Ragdoll cat is one of mutual respect, understanding, and love. Their affectionate nature and unique needs challenge us to be better caretakers and companions, making the journey one of the most rewarding experiences life has to offer. Embrace this opportunity to share your life with a Ragdoll cat, and you'll discover a bond that enriches your heart and home for years to come.